Ryan

Stanley

A ROOKIE READER

FAST DRAW
FREDDIE

by Bobbie Hamsa

Illustrations by Stephen Hayes

Prepared under the direction of Robert Hillerich, Ph.D.

CHILDRENS PRESS ™

CHICAGO

Library of Congress Cataloging in Publication Data

Hamsa, Bobbie.
    Fast draw Freddie.

    (A Rookie reader)
    Summary: Freddie draws all kinds of pictures fast:
big, small, fat, cat, and pictures of Mom and Dad too.
    [1. Drawing—Fiction.   2. Stories in rhyme]
I. Hayes, Steven, ill.   II. Title.   III. Series.
PZ8.3.H189Fas 1984   [E]   83-23931
ISBN 0-516-02045-5

Fast Draw Freddie draws pictures fast.

4

Big pictures.

Small pictures.

Short pictures.

Tall pictures.

Thin pictures.

Fat pictures.

Mouse pictures.

18

Cat pictures.

Pictures of Mom.

Pictures of Dad.

Pictures of Grandma that aren't too bad.

Get a pencil

CRAYONS

PENCILS

and a paper or two.

You can be a Fast Draw, too!

WORD LIST

a	mom
and	mouse
aren't	of
bad	or
be	paper
big	pencil
can	pictures
cat	short
dad	small
draw	tall
draws	that
fast	thin
fat	too
Freddie	two
get	you
grandma	

About the Author

Bobbie Hamsa was born and raised in Nebraska and has a Bachelor of Arts Degree in English Literature. She is an advertising copywriter for Bozell & Jacobs, Inc., writing print, radio, and television copy for many accounts, including "Mutual of Omaha's Wild Kingdom," the five-time Emmy Award winning wild animal series. She is the author of the popular series of books called Far-Fetched Pets, also published by Childrens Press. Bobbie lives in Omaha with her husband, Dick Sullivan, and children, John, Tracy, and Kenton.

About the Artist

Stephen Hayes is a free-lance, humorous illustrator from Cincinnati, Ohio. He received his degree in Fine Arts from Miami University in Oxford, Ohio. Steve has illustrated humorous greeting cards and several books for children. This book is dedicated to his wife, Susan, and his nine-month-old daughter, Sarah.